PORN, POETRY, & A GOD DAMN PEGASUS

A Collection of Bar Poems
By Fashion Joe

Illustrations By
Francesca Marina

Copyright © 2015 by Joseph Williams. All rights reserved

This book or any portion thereof may not be reproduced or used in any manner whatsoever without the express written permission of the publisher except for the use of brief quotations in articles and book reviews.

Any use of trademarked or copyrighted names of products or companies are used purely for descriptive purposes and are property of their rightful owners.

ISBN-10: 0996683402
ISBN-13: 978-0996683401

Illustrations by Francesca Marina

Contents

Porn, Poetry, And A God Damn Pegasus	2
Save The Trees	4
40 40 40	6
Shammu Man	8
Destiny	12
A Painted Evening	14
Glitter	16
The Nihilist	18
Drinking Alone	20
The Bar	22
The Whizzle	24
Gigolo Bo	28
Cybill Jo Sheen	30
Girl Power	32
Tig Bitties	36
Red	38
Santa Dreams	40
Euphemistic	42
21	44
The Truth Teller	48
An Evening Lunch	50
Veal	52
A Toast	54
Bills Bills Bills	56

Vicarious	58
Reconvene	60
Magnetism	62
The Angry Bull	66
Beelzebub's Tub	68
Music	70
Life Proofs	72
A Joyous Day	74
Fated Lovers	76
Wheel Chair Barbie	80
Juxtaposition	84
Excruciating	88
Lionel Coogle	92
Snow Days	94
Delicate Weeds	96
The Cat	98
The Need For Curry	100
A Delirious Thanksgiving	102
Confident Approach	104
Light Reading	106
The Cocked Face of Mr. Bones	108
Party	112
Entertainment	116
Fashion Joe	118
Practical Love	120
The Epic Stoner Poem	124

Introduction

Welcome one and all to the finest collection of poems that were once scribed on bar napkins, then later copied on to this fine fine paper, or transferred onto the series of 1's and 0's you see before you. It all really depends if you have a hard copy or digital copy. Either way, welcome!

This is a collection of satirical poems dedicated to man's relationships with love, self, nature, and booze. Also porn. Lots of porn. It's meant to rebel against romantics and the idea that poetry is just for those who develop raging boners for the succulent smell of lilacs, or those who pine for the love of a beautiful idiot. This is for the realists, or those who can at least see the humor in the fact that Trader Joe's does have the best curry.

Accompanied with these words are also illustrations that harken to a drunk Shel Silverstein, or a dirty Dr. Seuss. They are in a style of their own, but remind us of a time in which we gathered around the classroom, and sat entranced by those artists.

So get ready to sit back, enjoy a beer, and pray your mother doesn't walk in on you.

Porn, Poetry, And A God Damn Pegasus

Porn, Poetry, and a god damn Pegasus
The essential 3 P's to living
Besides Peeing
Possibly Peaking
And Painfully Pleading
Porn, Poetry and a god damn Pegasus

Porn, Poetry, And A God Damn Pegasus

Porn, Poetry, And A God Damn Pegasus

Save The Trees

Timid timbers of yorn
Downsized for use of porn
Never having realized their dreams
Now stuck as Penthouse Magazines

Once full of sticky sap
Man butter fills its gaps
Degraded and full of shame
Forced into promoting Jenna's fame

And to think of days past
Sitting idly in green green grass
Their futures were already deemed
To be used as an ends to filthy means

Porn, Poetry, And A God Damn Pegasus

Porn, Poetry, And A God Damn Pegasus

40 40 40

40 40 40
I gots ta get that 40
12 pack, stacked racks
Got to get that 40 shack
She wants the 40
She needs the 40
Oh my god
Oh my god
Me so horny
But she'll have to settle for a 22oz

Porn, Poetry, And A God Damn Pegasus

Shamu Man

Shamu man loved the trick ass hoes
He'd buy them rings
Diamond dreams
And rolls of doe
All to taste
Them thick ass folds

He loved the blubber
And would not stutter
"Bring on the butter."
He was sure to nut her

But then he met Pricilla
From the villa
And she knew the dilla
No spuge would a spilla

"Hey Shamu man!"
She would call
He was on his knees
And started to bawl

Porn, Poetry, And A God Damn Pegasus

"Whatchu want pretty thing?
I'll do it all
Hell I'd even lick your sugar wall."

She shook her head from side to side
"That ain't no way to get inside.
You need to be a man and full of pride.
If you wanna caress dem butt cheeks
And rub my thighs."

"Well what should I do
you pretty thang?"

"Get me Taco Bell
and I'll fuck ya plain."

And so she did...
While eating soft shell tacos

Porn, Poetry, And A God Damn Pegasus

Destiny

Is it fate that connects us?
Is there a driving force
Behind our lust?
Was our affair conceived
Before we knew?
Destiny predetermined, is it true?
I don't know
I'm just the milkman

Porn, Poetry, And A God Damn Pegasus

<u>Porn, Poetry, And A God Damn Pegasus</u>

A Painted Evening

Deep thoughts, deep nights,
Knee deep in pillow fights.
Show me them booty biscuits baby
And I'll drop the knot
And pop your top
Wtih sweet sugar locks.
Wearing frocks and smocks
I paint with rocks.
What's that?
Oh... Moaning Lisa.

Porn, Poetry, And A God Damn Pegasus

Glitter

Glitter on the dance floor
We know what it's for
Tonight's a special night
Bums ready for the knife fight

Everyone is dressed so dapper
Guns and amo?
Only knives to factor
Bums ready for the knife fight
And everything is feeling just right

Porn, Poetry, And A God Damn Pegasus

Porn, Poetry, And A God Damn Pegasus

The Nihilist

The lighthearted Nihilistic Caterer
Swiftly returned to nothing
Without a particular emotion
And lit a match to burn dimly
All he could think about were donuts

Porn, Poetry, And A God Damn Pegasus

Drinking Alone

Some say drinking alone is pathetic
I say...
Don't tell my mother

Porn, Poetry, And A God Damn Pegasus

The Bar

Vapor rises
From the moon lit glass
And glaciers swirl
From the pour so vast
The current reflects
Of experiences past
But all he feels is the love of last
The love so vibrant
He'd raise to mass
Thinking of those sweet boobies
And vivacious ass
But that time was gone
And from memory is cast
Along with used condoms
Stuck to his bed sheets

Porn, Poetry, And A God Damn Pegasus

Porn, Poetry, And A God Damn Pegasus

The Whizzle

The Whizzle sat upon a whizziling road
Down and dreary were his stories told
Lost love and fortune
Was all that was known
Until a Playboy he did own

He rose to his feet
And pecked at his meat
Soon rhythm and beats
Drove down his defeat

And all the while
Through nil and guile
A beast did file
Her grimly smile

She watched and waited
As time debated
Which stars were fated
Whiz masturbated

"Roar Roar!"
The beast had yelped
The Whizzle shrieked
"Come on baby!
Just need some help."

The beast had lain on all fours
Gels and oils spilled from her pores
And the Whizzle dreamt of ocean shores
As he fucked her on those dirty floors

Porn, Poetry, And A God Damn Pegasus

Porn, Poetry, And A God Damn Pegasus

Gigolo Bo

Full service
Bo shirtless
Felt worthless
As he shook his money maker

All for the dollar bills
All for the countless thrills
All to Amanda's will
That he be a booty shaker

He'd squiggle and wiggle
His belly would jiggle
For the countless giggles
As long as he could take her

But soon she tired
And why even bother
When love has expired
It's time to be a Quaker

Porn, Poetry, And A God Damn Pegasus

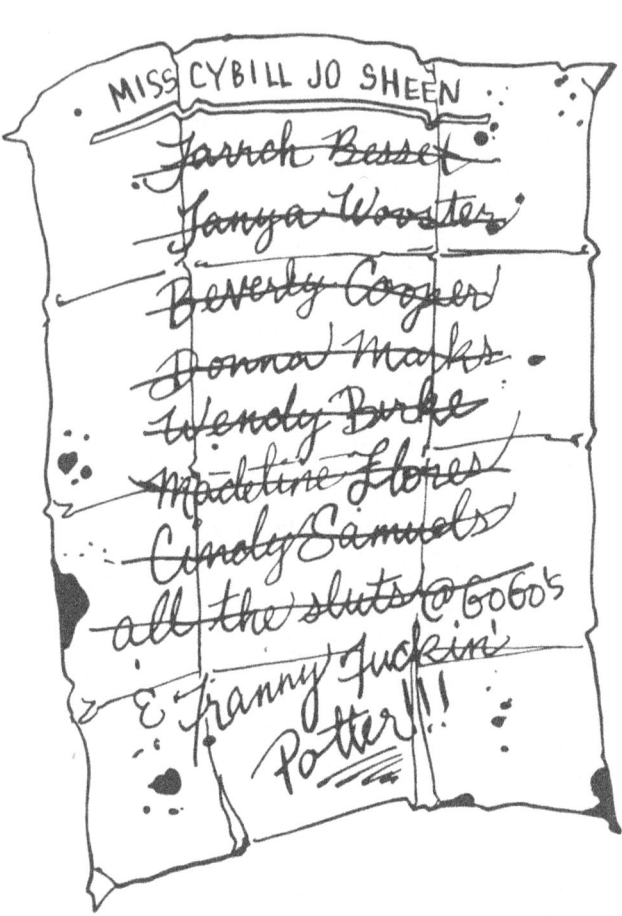

Porn, Poetry, And A God Damn Pegasus

Cybill Jo Sheen

Scribble dibble wibble,
Cybill willful of another dream
Pistol shit full with another magazine
Finger lingers as the passion triggers
One of her bright-eyed little schemes

Sinful pin pulled grenade alive it seems
Floating through the air
Destination unseen
One way or another her eyes do gleam
At the prospect of blowing that ass up
To little smithereens

And if there's a lesson
We find keen
Never steal a man
From Cybill Jo Sheen

Porn, Poetry, And A God Damn Pegasus

Girl Power

Girl Power Yo
Gots ta get that Girl Power
Nom saying?
Gotta stand up fo yo rights and shit
People just walk all over you
But that's when you stand up
And shout

"Mutha Fucka!
I gots that motha fuckin'
Girl Fuckin' Power
And I aint taking this shit no moe!
So sit dat cracker ass down
And I'ma tell you how it is.

#1 - I ain't yo maid,
And if you think
I'ma just pick up your shit,
You got another thing coming.

Porn, Poetry, And A God Damn Pegasus

#2- I know I gots a fine ass bun bun,
But if I catch you starring,
I'ma slap that toupee
Back into the rats nest
Where it came from.

And finally #3
The most mutha fuckin'
Important one of all.
I gots that Mutha Fuckin'
Girl Fuckin' Power,
And I aint taking this shit no moe!

Porn, Poetry, And A God Damn Pegasus

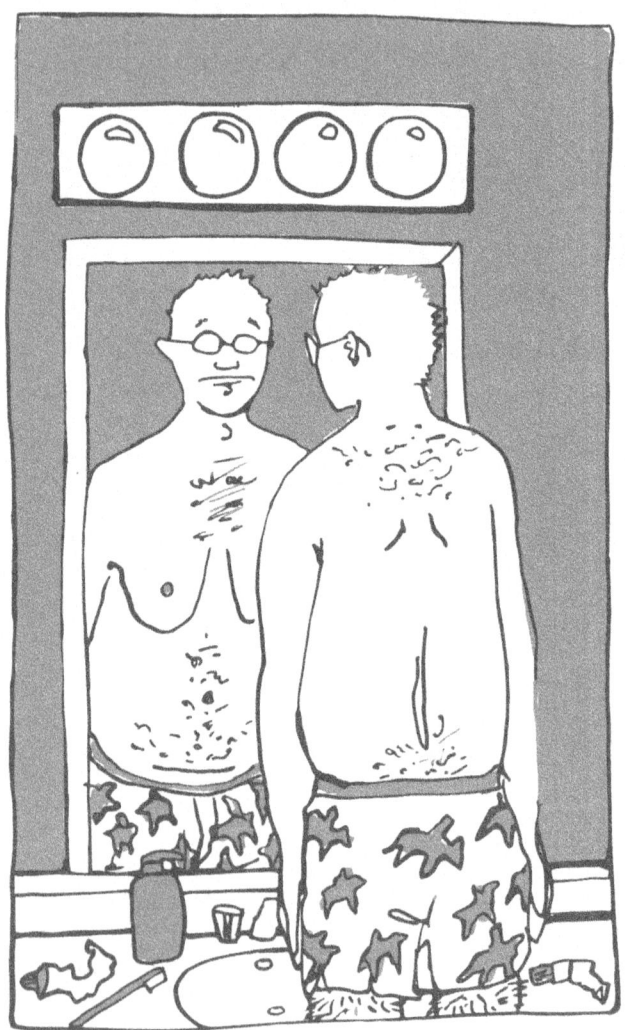

Porn, Poetry, And A God Damn Pegasus

Tig Bitties

How fat do you think my titties are?
No seriously,
How fat are my titties?
They gotta be C cups at least
Big ol' Titty C-bags
Is what they should call me
C-man Baggins from the
Lord of the Big Fat Titty Rings
It's pretty embarrassing
I mean
I drink a lot
I eat a lot
And some how I think
My titties won't conquer the world
So here we are
Smothered by my titty fat
Well ain't that a B!

Porn, Poetry, And A God Damn Pegasus

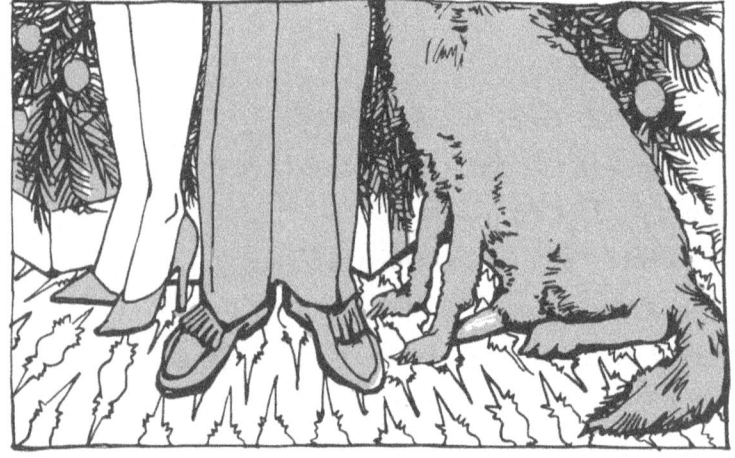

RED

It was red
Like... really red

My eyes were burning
As this dog was obviously yearning
I tried to keep my head from turning
But the image I was learning

He had passion in his eyes
As he showed off his big surprise
And no one could deny
That this dog
Loved obnoxious Christmas sweaters.

Porn, Poetry, And A God Damn Pegasus

Porn, Poetry, And A God Damn Pegasus

Santa Dreams

Santa
Sexy Santa
Secret Sexy Santa
Secretly into Santa
Into Man Santa
Man... love Santa

Porn, Poetry, And A God Damn Pegasus

Porn, Poetry, And A God Damn Pegasus

Euphemistic

Euphemistic
You and your linguistics
It's making my eyes stick
Like a hot load of Bisquick

Say that one again
About the glazed donut
I never laughed so hard
It made me blow nuts

I'd like to hear that all night long
While smoking your big fat bong
As the bells go ding and a dong
We could make that a hot new song

So why don't you pitch my tent
I've got some things to vent
It's ok, the pole is bent
I hear that feels better anyways.

Porn, Poetry, And A God Damn Pegasus

21

I'm 21
No seriously, I'm 21
It's super cool
I mean like, I can drink
Like legally drink
Oh my god, I got so wasted last night
Like super wasted
Like puking in my shoes wasted
And then taking a selfie in the shitter
Oh my god Becca, I was so wasted
And it was so awesome
It was so so awesome
Like super awesome
If I could just take a selfie
In the shitter every night
I'd be so so happy
Is that a beer?
Becca, is that a beer?
Gimmie that beer Becca!
I need to take a shit
No seriously Becca gimmie that beer
I need to take a shit

Porn, Poetry, And A God Damn Pegasus

Becca, I am 21
And if I tell you to give me that beer
So I can take a shit
You are legally
By law
Supposed to give me that beer
So give me that god damn beer Becca!

<u>Porn, Poetry, And A God Damn Pegasus</u>

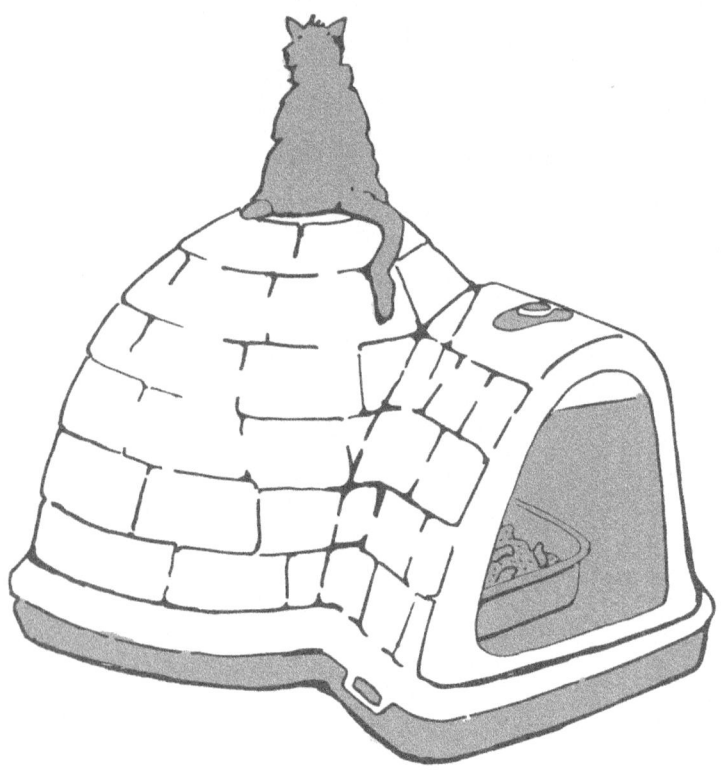

Porn, Poetry, And A God Damn Pegasus

The Truth Teller

Constantly **C**rowded
Anxiously **A**nointed
Truth **T**eller

Sells **S**hort
His **H**ummus
Inside **I**gloos
To **T**ell
Sobering **S**tories

Before **B**erating
Rowdy **R**oosters
Ovulating **O**penly

Porn, Poetry, And A God Damn Pegasus

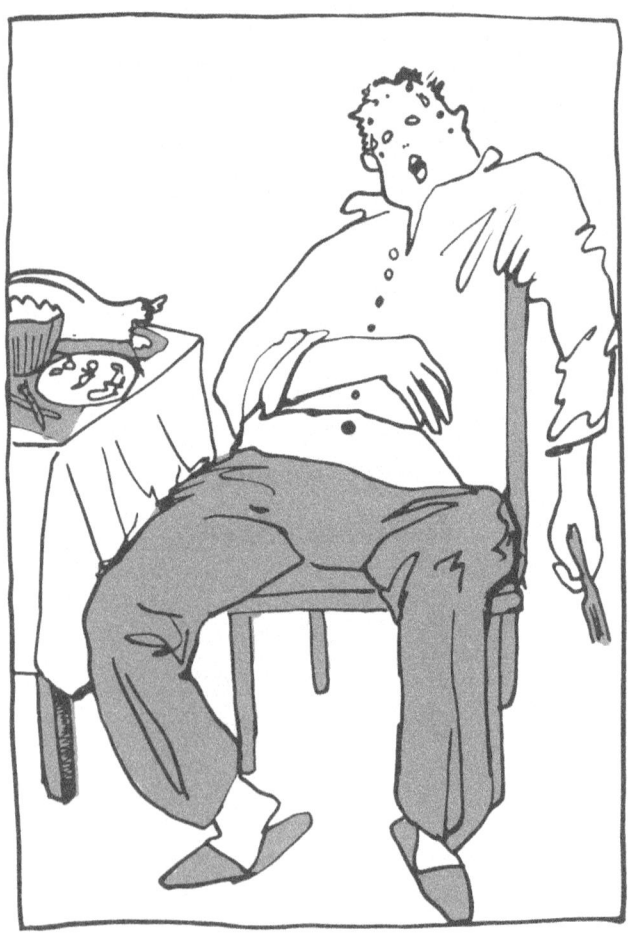

An Evening Lunch

Stuffed like a potato
I feel the swelling
Belly bulging
Loins sweating
Where are a good pair of sweatpants
When you need them?

Porn, Poetry, And A God Damn Pegasus

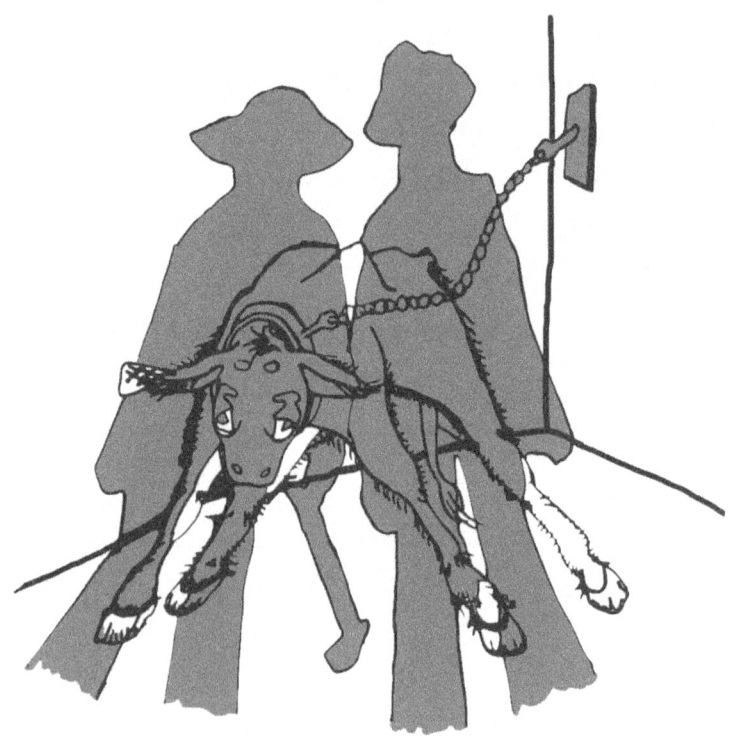

Veal

Open mouth pursed
Here comes that veal baby
It's supple like bounded thighs
Slab on a concrete of butter
Is that a side of honey glaze?
Veal baby, yeah!
Chomp those cheeks
Let it dribble
It's veal baby
Eat as much as you please
Tear into that skin
It's new
Don't you like eating veal baby?
Fuck that tofu shit
I'm going to eat a baby

Porn, Poetry, And A God Damn Pegasus

A Toast

It stands crispy and tall
Proud of its flakes
It browns more

Taking in heat
Transforming moods that are meek
Truly a defender of the weak

It's toast my good man
And it would brighten up anyone
Who held it in their hand

But alas our story is grim
For the item dubbed toaster
Its lights are dim
And we can't afford a new one

Porn, Poetry, And A God Damn Pegasus

Bills Bills Bills

Bills bills bills
Look at all dem bills
Lord Jesus have mercy
I don't know what to do
Wit all dem bills
Thay's more bills than I can count
It's impossible for me to keep track
Of all dees bills
Who knew
So many ducks swam at this pond?

Porn, Poetry, And A God Damn Pegasus

Porn, Poetry, And A God Damn Pegasus

Vicarious

To enjoy my life
I vicariously live
Through tiny turtles

<u>Porn, Poetry, And A God Damn Pegasus</u>

Porn, Poetry, And A God Damn Pegasus

Reconvene

Re-con-vene
Be ob-scene
Eat fun beans
Heat bun please
Pee sun beams
See cubs dream
Me dumb tree
He shuns thee
So let us
Re-con-vene
At a later date...
How about Tuesday?

Porn, Poetry, And A God Damn Pegasus

Porn, Poetry, And A God Damn Pegasus

Magnetism

I feel like there's a connection
Disregarding our complication
And the need to please convention
I sense a light love tension

Now you've got your golden lock hair
And your open chest to bare
And I can't help but stare
As I'm sitting way over there

But you flash your smile
My heart thumps for a while
I can't resist that sort of style
It's something to put away in my file

You come over to caress my chest
Rubbing and pleasing it is the best
Oh those hands surely pass the test
So I start wagging my tail
From east to west

Porn, Poetry, And A God Damn Pegasus

You say, "You're a good boy."
And you bought me a new toy
But an English man comes up and says
"Oiy!
Get your hands off my fucking dog!"

Porn, Poetry, And A God Damn Pegasus

<u>Porn, Poetry, And A God Damn Pegasus</u>

The Angry Bull

The rattled cattle
Battled my paddle
For about an hour
But then he drowned

Porn, Poetry, And A God Damn Pegasus

Porn, Poetry, And A God Damn Pegasus

Beelzebub's Tub

Beelzebub
Getting ready for the bath tub
Drumming up those soapy suds
So fresh and clean like a super stud
Crazy loud, he hears a thud
Dashes out to see what's up
His mother on the ground
She passed swiftly into the night

Porn, Poetry, And A God Damn Pegasus

Music

Rhythmic pulses bring life
Freedom releases
I sit in solitude
But the outside world continually knocks
I find myself compelled to reply
And I do
But I sure take my sweet ass time

Porn, Poetry, And A God Damn Pegasus

Life Proofs

Now if I have my shirt put on
I'll have put on my shirt
If I have a trip that I've gone
I'll have gone on that trip
And if it's wine that I drank
Then I have drank at Olive Garden

Porn, Poetry, And A God Damn Pegasus

Porn, Poetry, And A God Damn Pegasus

A Joyous Day

The Boy Toy had Joy
As he danced with Billy's frilly lilies
And sang a new June tune
Around noon on a Saturday
This is the story of how Harrison Ford
Was cast to play Han Solo

Porn, Poetry, And A God Damn Pegasus

ONLINE DATE.COM

KENNETH PLENNET
FLAGSTAFF AZ, 29

LIKES	DISLIKES
ICE CREAM	FAT FREE YOGURT
BONING	LOW THREAD COUNT SHEETS
TUPAC	UPTIGHT BITCHES

Fated Lovers

It is in the stars
That we must bang so heartedly
That my throbbing member
Defile your grace
In the most mysterious of ways

One of which will be missionary

And "YAY!" you will shout
"Praise be to the stars
That fated us so,
For without thine penis
My flower would wilt foe show."

"Yes my lady."
I shall whisper back

"But for now
I must rest my sack
To raise an army
That will infiltrate said ass."

Thirty minutes shall pass
And the passion will be plentiful
As if no intermission had ever occurred
Ecstasy will fill your lungs
As I clasp onto those vivacious buns
And hum a melody Tupac has sung

Cringing with delight
You convulse to taste
My spermy waste
And I shall abide
Eating ice cream all the while
For I most enjoy the Breyers

When mornings light caresses your skin
You will find me likened to a lycan
A hairy man beast
That you still want to sex
And yay, I shall comply
With the most devious smile
And heavy load to pile
Your will in no denial
Shall except the cum
That I just fucking unloaded

Porn, Poetry, And A God Damn Pegasus

Wheel Chair Barbie

She's my... Wheel Chair Barbie
10 out of 10 hardly
Try 10 million out of one to start B

Her platinum hair
Shimmers down to her chair
Chrome wheels glisten and flare
Beneath sunlight's glare
And I do declare
My arousal from skin so fair
Her bosoms so bare
I would even dare
To bask in her booby lair

Lips red with passion
Dressed in latest fashions
My heart need not ration
For this girl I want to blast in

Porn, Poetry, And A God Damn Pegasus

Eyes of silk
Voice as milk
Arms so built
My seed has spilt

She's my... Wheel Chair Barbie
10 out of 10 hardly
Try 10 million out of one to start B
And to think we met at Arby's

Porn, Poetry, And A God Damn Pegasus

Porn, Poetry, And A God Damn Pegasus

Juxtaposition

When you juxtapose
Two of those
I suppose hoes
It's important he knows
Which of these does
Comes with free blow

It's not for him
More a blood of kin
Who hurt his shin
From walking into a paper bin
I know I know, a little dim

But his name is Jerry
And I think he'd like Cherri
If there's cocaine he'd be merry
Otherwise Betty's kind of scary
Wouldn't a dog be less hairy?
And, oh my God, is she leaking dairy?

Porn, Poetry, And A God Damn Pegasus

So Betty's who he'll get?
Well this deadline needs to be met
And if it will clear my debt
I'll take Betty but first
We'll take her to a vet

Porn, Poetry, And A God Damn Pegasus

Excruciating

Is that a cactus up your ass!
Now why did you have to be so crass
We were just fishing for bass
And you shoved it up so fast

I don't know what you want me to do
I ain't going there for you
I thought it was weird, all the lube
And that 2x4 cylinder tube

A new fishing technique I thought
With all that crazy shit you bought
Or old family secret you were taught
But now your butt is going to clot

Why must you ruin this for me
A quiet morning fishing by the sea
Nothing to do but relax and dream
And drink a beer, two, or three

Porn, Poetry, And A God Damn Pegasus

Now don't take my pliers
Oh great, now I'll set them on fire
Isn't there a doctor you can hire
That's something rather dire

Oh boy here it comes
Well this trip sure was fun
After this you and I are done
There will be no ass cactuses
In the bum

Porn, Poetry, And A God Damn Pegasus

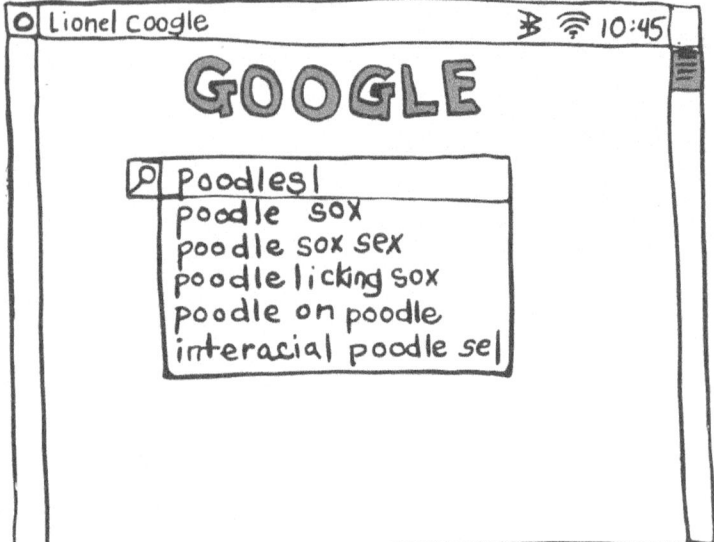

Porn, Poetry, And A God Damn Pegasus

Lionel Coogle

Lionel Coogle
Decided to google
How to doodle
Pasta Roni noodles
Then kanoodled
With his wife's poodle

The feds were quick
To arrive on the scene

Porn, Poetry, And A God Damn Pegasus

Porn, Poetry, And A God Damn Pegasus

Snow Days

Gangsters in the snow
Dancing through their woes
Happy grins on their faces
No more drugs or beer cases
Cheeks turning red
Today no one is dead
They hug and laugh
And impersonate Shaft
It's a snowy day
And everything's A.O.K.

Porn, Poetry, And A God Damn Pegasus

Delicate Weeds

Dainty dandelions demand
Dignified disses while
Dancing distastefully at Denny's

Porn, Poetry, And A God Damn Pegasus

The Cat

With a laser beam
Fighting off robot fiends
Sipping on some ginseng
Now at the age of thirteen

He has a samurai chop
Likes listening to hip hop
His respirator goes bip bop
He's the cat in the flip flops

Porn, Poetry, And A God Damn Pegasus

The Need For Curry

He roamed the mountains
And traveled distant seas
In search of the perfect curry
His taste buds did need

He explored India, Thailand,
Pakistan, and France
But no curry made him leap with joy
And do a little dance

Suddenly his eyes did behold
The perfect curry
With flavors to unfold

It seemed so obvious
And now he knows
The best damn curry
Is at Trader Joes

Porn, Poetry, And A God Damn Pegasus

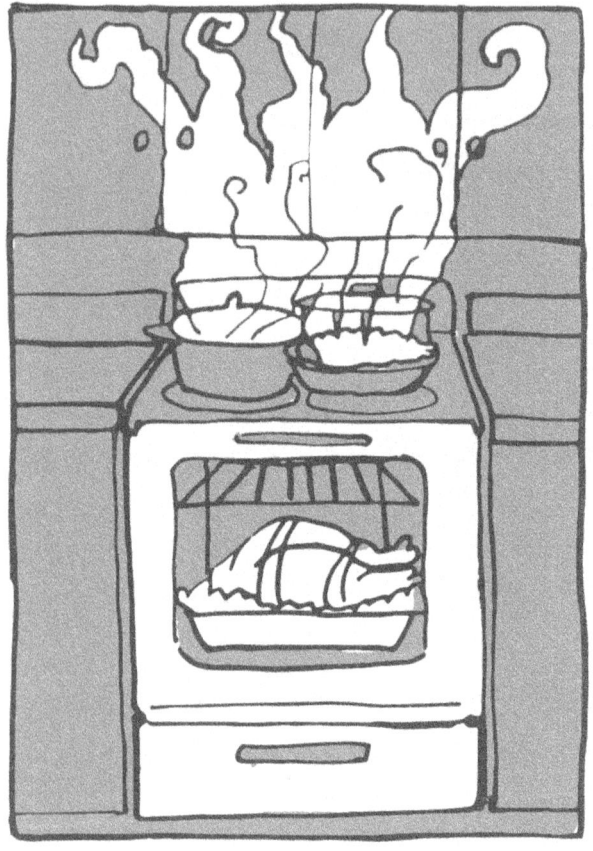

A Delirious Thanksgiving

Oh boy I'm so hot
So hot and sweaty
I'm drippin' gravy
My mind has gone delirious

Lord have mercy it's hot
My skin is baking
Feeling innards shaking
My mind has gone delirious

H. E. double hockey sticks it's hot!
Things is looking murky
Why God am I a turkey
My mind has gone delirious

Porn, Poetry, And A God Damn Pegasus

Porn, Poetry, And A God Damn Pegasus

Confident Approach

When I'm lost
I flail my arms like a quail
Stranded in the pale
Blue light sun
I prevail
Flappity flap
Go my wings taking sail
Suddenly I burst
Out of my shell
Everything is bright
As far as I can tell
Reaching for the sky
Nothing else compels
My spirit flies forth
Out of this well
Did I get her number?
No, I got Taco Bell

Porn, Poetry, And A God Damn Pegasus

Light Reading

Lathered in Coppertones
Latest sun protective lotion
He sat quietly in his room
Bathed in the light reflected
From the pages of a novel
A friend had wrote

SPF 30 would do.

Porn, Poetry, And A God Damn Pegasus

Porn, Poetry, And A God Damn Pegasus

The Cocked Face of Mr. Bones

Bones was a man
A man who would cock
His rumpeled forehead
At anything that mooned his mother
On a Tuesday eve

And on one particular Tuesday
He noted a swamp of skimpy school fish
Scuttering about his kitchen floor
They flopped and flageled
In front of Bones's mother

And Harry
The leader of the pack
Who was native born of Mexico
Dropped his scaly feathers
Thus exposing his finely oiled salmon ass
And shook about violently
Parading his ass for all to see

Porn, Poetry, And A God Damn Pegasus

Needless to say
Bones was very disturbed by this image
And he proceeded to cock his head
In an unruly manner

Bones had had enough
And wanted no more to do
With these practical pranksters
So he pulled out his shotgun
And shot his mother in the face

Point blank

Harry's playful smile faded
And turned into a pale
Blue vat of emptiness
He had nothing more to live for

Porn, Poetry, And A God Damn Pegasus

Porn, Poetry, And A God Damn Pegasus

Party

Flashing lights
Crazy nights
Drinking Sprite
Outta site

Non caffeinated buzz
I knew where I was
Chillin' with the cuz
Playing with my chin fuzz

The beat was thumping
And we was jumping
A girl came rumping
And started humping

We got down
To another town
We weren't around
For her to blow us now

Party Nights!
Party Days!
We like to Party!
In sober ways!

Porn, Poetry, And A God Damn Pegasus

Entertainment

Step right up
Step right up
And take a shot
At winning this gold plated duck
Wouldn't you like to have this mallard?
I swear to God
He's not a health hazard
He died of natural causes
So we covered him in gold
To console our losses
And now he can be yours
At the cost of a dime
You better hurry up now
Cause we're running out of time

Just take the damn thing!

Porn, Poetry, And A God Damn Pegasus

Fashion Joe

He sailed the seas
With relative ease
And all to please
Some big titties

"I must save those tits."

Porn, Poetry, And A God Damn Pegasus

Porn, Poetry, And A God Damn Pegasus

Practical Love

Have I not earned the right
To love you illogically?
To profess form tongue irresponsibly?
To yodel through air undeniably?
To traverse terrain triumphantly?

There is no reason
This season
To pleasing
Yet I believe in
This love despite its treason
Or its appearance of such a state

And for its sake
The effect at stake
Is to inspire warmth not hate
For I long for your embrace
And in face
Lick your lips of lace
Tickle behind ears with good taste
And maybe one day mate

Porn, Poetry, And A God Damn Pegasus

I do not expect you to melt
From words of woo
But I desire to be felt
And hopefully so do you

So let it be known
My thoughts on this affair
And this burden I air
In hopes for you to bare
My children's balding hair

Porn, Poetry, And A God Damn Pegasus

Porn, Poetry, And A God Damn Pegasus

The Epic Stoner Poem

The local Bogal
Smoked a tokefull
chokefull bowl
In hopes pull, to the right direction
But what he found
So profound
The sound of coughing
Sent his soul jaunting
And he was too high to pick up the mail

In this tale
Our hero fails
Mother's expectations
To great exaltations
But be bothered not
By Burty Bogal's pot
Smoking,
As it all changes in the second act

Porn, Poetry, And A God Damn Pegasus

Though trapped
By his addictive knacks
The facts stacked
Should he get notice
Of bills shouting "Owe us!"
He'd remain tokeless
And homeless
His prosthetic leg would be clothesless
So he waited

No longer faded
Obviously not elated
The jaded berated man
Without a tan
Ran to the porch
Where his skin doth torch
In search of letters
But mainly weather
Drove him back
To the comfort of his home

Burned to bone
Bogal burned to stoned
Forgetting the troubles
And bulging puss bubbles
Freshly formed on his flesh
Flaccidly he slept
Dreaming of those dastardly debts
That kept him
From vacationing in Uganda

Blasting Jane Fonda
Arose his senses kinda
But noticing Larry
And his gay friend Terry
Exercising merrily
Mostly mustard his ability to wake up

"Hey Bogal
Why so woeful?"
Larry asked soulful

Bogal in a loathful state
But knowing of Larry's good faith
Responded kindly to Larry and his mate
That mail he needed to take
Still sat upon the stoop so late
But he had been so baked
His mind would quake
At the idea of getting up

"Well that's just lazy
You crazy hazy looking man.
Stop smoking so much
And get your shit together, damn!"

Affected by Larry's words
Bogal rose to take a turd
And would sit for fifteen minutes
Contemplating mental limits
And whether or not
Larry would witness
Bogal going to the mailbox

Porn, Poetry, And A God Damn Pegasus

Determined to no longer fail
Having run out of weed
He exhaled
And with a new wind
He would prove to his kin
That he could at least
Pay the electric bill

He charged with all his might
Forgetting his pants in flight
To the front door
Where he could explore
More or less
The outside world

Finally aiming to finish chores
He marched outside
Full of pride
He'd bend down in stride
Only to see flashing lights surprise him

Blue and Red
Filled with dread
Bogal knew instead
What was going to happen
And with fractions
Of seconds for reaction
He soon was latched in
Chains and escorted off
By the authority figures

He'd never know
Of the bills he'd owe
But instead was towed
For nudity exposed
And getting stoned
For days alone
Had only added to his tragic end

BIOS

Fashion Joe started his writing career in the 4th grade when he wrote a short story about a monkey who wears a diaper. And due to the high marks he received as a child, he continued to write more. He quickly transitioned to topics of sex, booze, and food, all of which he was familiar with at an early age, but his teachers stopped praising his work and urged him to seek council instead. "Fashion" then went super saiyan, and hadoukened his way towards freedom of expression.

Francesca picked up the quill and ink the very moment Fashion Joe started spitting sick sonnets. The two friends met the "old-fashioned" way, at a bar, and planned from the get go to create a world of art and nonsense that non senselessly makes cents.

Francesca, or "Frankie" for short, is a classically trained oil painter and loves to create the largest biggest scariest paintings of mountains and militia to let the world know she may have lived on another planet. Joe's poems literary spoke to Frankie and she talked back with black. The images you see now are the created references for the world of Fashion Joe. Voila!

www.ingramcontent.com/pod-product-compliance
Lightning Source LLC
Chambersburg PA
CBHW032135040426
42449CB00005B/249